the TROUBLE with Paris

Following Jesus in a World of Plastic Promises

The TROUBLE with Paris

Following Jesus in a World of Plastic Promises

Mark Sayers

NASHVILLE   DALLAS   MEXICO CITY   RIO DE JANEIRO   BEIJING

© 2008 by Mark Sayers

The publishers are grateful to Cameron Conant for his collaboration and writing skills in developing the content of this book.

All rights reserved. No portion of this book may be reproduced, stored in a retrieval system, or transmitted in any form or by any means—electronic, mechanical, photocopy, recording, scanning, or other—except for brief quotations in critical reviews or articles, without the prior written permission of the publisher.

Published in Nashville, Tennessee, by Thomas Nelson. Thomas Nelson is a trademark of Thomas Nelson, Inc.

Thomas Nelson, Inc. titles may be purchased in bulk for educational, business, fund-raising, or sales promotional use. For information, please e-mail SpecialMarkets@ThomasNelson.com.

Scripture marked Voice is taken from The Voice™ translation. Copyright © 2006, 2007, 2008 by Ecclesia Bible Society. Used by permission. All rights reserved.

Scripture marked KJV is from The Holy Bible, King James Version.

ISBN 978-1-4185-3339-7

Printed in the United States of America

08 09 10 11 12 RRD 6 5 4 3 2 1

Week One: The Trouble with Hyperreality — 7

Week Two: The Trouble with Celebrity — 33

Week Three: The Trouble with Entertainment — 55

Week Four: The Promise of God's Reality — 81

Quoted Resources — 105

The Trouble with Hyperreality

An Introduction to Week One

Las Vegas is a city of entertainment, sex, shopping, and gambling—a place where dreams come true... or so we're told. In Las Vegas, you can gamble with celebrities, sunbathe with beautiful people, and eat dinner at the top of the Eiffel Tower—or something that looks like the Eiffel Tower—before heading to "New York" for a "Broadway show."

In Las Vegas, you can shop at the trendiest boutiques during the day and party like a rock star at night. And "what happens in Vegas, stays in Vegas," the marketing slogan goes. It's as if visitors are told, "Do what you want; no one has to know. This isn't real anyway." But when French philosopher Jean Baudrillard visited Las Vegas, he didn't call it unreal—he called it *hyperreal*. When you think about it, his point really wasn't so different from what Las Vegas marketers might say.

Hyperreality is the condition in which artificial stimulation is preferable to interaction with reality. As U2 sings, it's "even better than the real thing." And that's exactly what's for sale in Las Vegas—the "authentic fake." It's just like the real thing, only "better."

So perhaps it's not surprising that in hyperreality, you are defined not by your character, but by your cell phone, clothes, car, looks, and house. In hyperreality, you are what you consume, because what you consume says something about you. In such a world, a eulogy might sound something like this: "Eric wore Adidas, he loved Starbucks, he dated supermodels, he drove a Mercedes, and he always used American Express."

Based on his preferences, we can only conclude that Eric was an upwardly mobile fellow, clearly a man of taste. But if we step outside of hyperreality, we really know nothing about Eric based on that description. And that's exactly the point. For Baudrillard, reality is dead, and in our increasingly global, technological world, hyperreality is as close as we can get to the real thing.

If this is true, what does it mean for people who are trying to follow Jesus?

It's a perplexing question, especially in a world where consumerism has replaced religion. Just look at some of the words marketers use in their advertisements; for example, *intimate*, *mystery*, and *warmth*. If we take our cues from the global media, it would appear that a transcendent experience with the divine is no longer necessary. What we *really* need is a trip to the luxury car dealership, or an in-person encounter with a celebrity.

That's because in hyperreality, transcendence is achieved through improving one's image—a futile pursuit that ends in anxiety and frustration. The perfect image is forever just out of reach because there is always something new to buy, or a new celebrity to worship. But it's difficult not to chase after these things in a culture that maintains that these things are the means by which we achieve nirvana.

However, in hyperreality, all is not as it seems. Cherry cola tastes nothing like cherries, and airbrushed models are not the glamorous girls we imagine them to be—all of which leads one to ask, "What is real, and what isn't?" In today's world, the line between reality and fantasy is increasingly blurred—and in many cases, obliterated entirely.

- Play DVD.

- Turn the page and follow along with the DVD.

- Discussion questions are at the end of the session.

The Trouble with Hyperreality

Promises That Don't Deliver

Ben Catford remembers the moment that changed his life. Young and successful, Ben was a public relations consultant at a big firm. He spent his days working with rock stars, his nights partying with celebrities.

One day, backstage at a concert, Ben watched one of the world's biggest stars leave the stage, to the applause of forty thousand adoring fans. A ball of energy on-stage, that famous musician now sat down, alone, and looked off into the distance, seemingly bored and depressed. He went from rock god to no one in particular in a matter of moments. Pop culture is like that: it promises the world, but when the noise dies down, it leaves us surprisingly empty. It's sort of like filling our stomachs with chocolate bars. They

taste great, but they are full of empty calories and eventually leave us wanting something more—which begs the question: When we have lost our faith in pop culture—when chocolate bars will no longer do—where can we turn for substance, for something truly filling?

A Shiny, Hopeful Future?

Consider this:

- Standards of living have never been higher.

- Technology offers a vision of a shiny, hopeful future.

- We are living longer than our grandparents and great-grandparents.

Yet despite our high standard of living and the utopian promises of technology, many of us feel as if our lives are lacking—as if the good life is just out of reach. Though we are wealthier than most of the world, many Westerners feel a gnawing sense of discontentment. And for those of us trying to follow Jesus, things get even more complicated. If we are going to live as Christians in this age, we have to understand the times and how they are radically altering the way we think, behave, and live.

Welcome to Hyperreality, Where...

- It's hard to distinguish the real from the imaginary.

- Cherry cola doesn't taste like cherries.

- Pornography is nothing like real sex.

- You are told that, to be happy, you have to reach for the superficial—the fake.

"In this 'simulated' world, images become objects, rather than reflecting them; reality becomes Hyper-Reality. In Hyper-Reality it is no longer possible to distinguish the imaginary from the real . . . the true from the false."

—Krishan Kumar

A Suburban Teenage Mother—and a European Fashion Model

I once met a suburban teenage mother—a girl who had been through a fair number of trials in her life. During our conversation, I learned that she was a model and had even been featured in top European fashion magazines, and she had the photos to prove it, glossy snapshots that transformed her into the kind of woman every other woman wanted to be—and every man wanted to be with. The kind of woman you'd see on the French Riviera and on dates with Italian race car drivers. But the glamorous life of a top fashion model bore little resemblance to the girl I saw before me. It was hyperreality at its best.

Many of us see this in our everyday lives as well. MySpace or Facebook photos—taken from the perfect angle in the perfect light—often bear little resemblance to their subject, the man or woman we would meet in person. In hyperreality, we can create a persona, or personas, of our choosing. In fact, some people have several online personalities, each attracting its own distinct following. Take for example a woman who confessed to keeping three separate blogs, with each online journal painting a very different picture of who she was. In hyperreality, words and images are not vehicles by which truth is conveyed, but rather tools to create "truth" as we see fit.

You Are What You Consume

People were once known for what they produced, and they took pride in the goods and services they delivered. But today people are increasingly removed from the means of production—in fact, few of us even know where our *food* comes from; we just know it arrived at the supermarket. Today, people are known for what they consume, not what they produce, and in hyperreality, there are layers of meaning ascribed to what we consume.

For example:

- A chocolate bar can make you more attractive to the opposite sex.

- The brand of diapers you buy determines how caring a parent you are.

- A certain cell phone can introduce you to a hip new set of friends.

- A vacation overseas gives your life meaning.

- A particular car improves your standing in society.

Look at the ways we pay homage to consumerism. Christmas—once a religious celebration of the birth of Jesus—is now the season retailers depend upon to meet their yearly sales goals. And after the holiday, the first question out of people's mouths is typically not, "How did you celebrate the birth of Christ?" but rather, "What did you get for Christmas?" And make no mistake: what you got for Christmas is of more importance to most than how you practiced your faith. In our world, buying things, not worshiping a deity, is the true way to achieve meaning.

"Consumption is . . . the healer, the caretaker, the lover, the spiritual, the feeder, and the consolation. It is the chief rival to God in our culture."

—Alan Storkey

Advertising: The Language of Religion

Advertising now uses the language of religion: words like *intimacy*, *sensuality*, *mystery*, *warmth*. Purchase the right clothes and you can be a meaning maker. Buy the right computer and you can be a revolutionary. In fact, Apple would have you believe that buying a MacBook Pro will turn you into an out-of-the-box creative destined to change the world; Victoria's Secret would have you believe that their lingerie will turn women into seductive angels; and Nike wants you to know—whether you're an athlete or not—that their shoes instill courage and perseverance. All of this language affects us at a profound, heart level. Humans are spiritual beings, and the words used in advertisements today often touch us at our spiritual core, creating confusion about what true spirituality even looks like.

Our Purchases, Our Identity

In today's world, we are told that our purchases are not just functional—they send messages about our social status and identity. Buying a house in a particular neighborhood says something about you, as does buying a specific dog food. And you do want to be a high-end, discerning purchaser of dog food, don't you?

It is interesting how marketers are always on the lookout for people they call "trendsetters": those considered purveyors of "cool." Marketers figure that if you can reach the trendsetters with a product, and they like it, others will surely follow. And who are the trendsetters today? Often, they're celebrities. That's why marketers fight to get their products included in gift baskets for celebrity awards shows, and why they give away clothes that they know will be worn on the red carpet.

The underlying message is that wearing this dress or using that product will make you cool, because, "Look, the trendsetters wear/use it!" And if you don't feel cool, your credit card can fix that. At least that's the promise of consumerism.

Sell Yourself

Consumerism has hijacked all aspects of everyday life: politics, parenting, religion, and relationships are all consumer exchanges. The Western adult is the supreme shopper, remaining noncommittal while looking for the best deal. In hyperreality, this attitude particularly impacts our view of sex. In hyperreality:

- You must have the right look and the right partner.

- Partners are accessories, and there is little commitment.

- Your body is a storefront, and sex is the product.

Online dating has made this particularly true. Searching for a date online bears striking resemblance to shopping for a car at an auto dealership. The shopper often knows little about the engine, but is very much attracted to the color and shape of the car.

"Ideally, nothing should be embraced by a consumer firmly, nothing should command a commitment 'til death do us part.' . . . There ought to be a proviso 'until further notice' attached to any oath of loyalty and commitment."

—Zygmunt Bauman

Judging a Book by Its Cover

Today we judge people by their exteriors, not by their character. This explains why the weight-loss industry is booming, cosmetic surgeries are at an all-time high, and fashions change at such a rapid rate. We believe that if we can just change the outside, meaning and happiness will follow. This notion is fed by the global media, which produces hyperreal images at a dizzying rate. And it's against these hyperreal images that we judge our appearance and social standing. So much of our discontent comes from comparing ourselves to the models we see in advertising. The problem is that it's hard to trust these images. In our technological world, everything is recolored and touched up. Are we even seeing the real model in a photograph? Or are we seeing an artist's conception of that model? Whatever the case, such unrealistic images feed us a hyperreal vision of what our clothes, bodies, and lives should look like—a vision that is unattainable.

"The modern individual within the consumer culture . . . speaks not only with his clothes, but with his home, furnishings, decorations, car, and other activities."

—Mike Featherstone

Everything Is an Accessory

Spirituality in the West is something like shopping at a supermarket—for many, it's an accessory rather than a life commitment. There are even online quizzes designed to help you determine which religion is right for you, as if, again, spirituality is not truth to be discovered, but an accessory to be added to your life . . . that is, if it's convenient.

This isn't entirely a contemporary problem. We need only look at the Old Testament to see how people have always given up the good things God gives them in exchange for false promises, idols, and delusions. While the delusions have taken different shapes and forms over the centuries—a golden calf, the Tower of Babel, or any number of other lies we have fallen for—our attraction to them seems almost a part of the human condition. This week, look to knock down the delusions in our hyperreal world, a world that tries to get us to accept something that appears to be more, but is significantly less than the real thing.

Discussion Questions

1 What examples of hyperreality have you seen in the culture around you? How are you personally tempted by the promises of hyperreality?

2 Think of the products you have bought in the last six months (clothing, DVDs, etc.). If you were to dig deeply, what emotions motivated you to buy these products?

3   Was there a time when you felt you had "made it"? How long did the feeling last? Why do you think the feeling went away?

4   What messages are you trying to communicate to others through the products you buy? As you consider this question, what specific products—and the "lifestyles" their marketing promises—come to mind?

Discussion

5 How has the framework of consumerism affected your view of commitment?

6 How have you seen consumerism affecting religion in the culture around you?

7 The term "church shopping" is often used today to refer to the process of looking for the "perfect" church. What are the underlying values and ideas behind this term? Are you a church shopper?

8 What stood out to you in this session? Go around the group and share.

9 What personal questions did this session raise for you?

The TROUBLE with Celebrity

An Introduction to Week Two

Before getting started with Week Two, spend some time reviewing "Week One: The Trouble with Hyperreality." Discuss with your group some examples of hyperreality that each of you observed during the past week.

With all of the television shows and magazines dedicated to the rich and famous, it's hard to not want to live like a celebrity these days. And for much of the Western world, the celebrity lifestyle is within reach. Even on a modest salary, I can afford an iPhone, an iPod, a MacBook, a rented duplex in a hip part of town, a leased luxury car, and the occasional vacation to an exotic locale.

Trips to the high-end salon or purchases from the trendy boutique aren't out of the question either. In other words, I can buy my way to celebrity status . . . sort of. With the right attitude and clothes, I can literally walk into certain restaurants and coffee shops and have others think that maybe—just maybe—I'm someone important: perhaps a red-carpet celebrity in disguise, or an indie musician on the verge of an artistic breakthrough.

Heck, I *can* be a celebrity if I want. We've fulfilled Andy Warhol's vision of a world where everyone is famous for fifteen minutes. Reality shows parade across our television screens, YouTube turns students and stay-at-home moms into overnight sensations, and blogs allow aspiring writers to be read by hundreds, even thousands of people per day. But if you're not satisfied with the number of people reading your blog or listening to your band's demo on MySpace or YouTube, there are other ways to get attention.

Let me tell you a story: maybe the one about my three-month trip to Europe, or the college semester I spent in Paris, or the trip I'm planning to Beijing. After all, if I can't be a celebrity in today's world, the next best thing is to have a bunch of cool experiences to discuss.

Me at a Party: Yeah, that reminds me of when I was in Budapest . . .

Attractive Member of the Opposite Sex Standing Close to Me at a Party: You went to Budapest? Wow! Tell me about it . . .

Suddenly, I'm not just another guy; I'm the guy who knows the ins and outs of Budapest.

Marketers know that in today's hyperreal world, cool experiences are more important than ever, so we're promised not just a cruise, but an adventure; not just a backpacking trip, but self-discovery. Hyperreality's triune god could be said to be luxury items, celebrity status, and cool experiences—three in one, with each part of this strange trinity providing, as Christopher Lasch has said, "the momentary illusion of personal well-being, health, and psychic security." Emphasis on the word *momentary*.

And speaking of momentary, how about death? We aren't on this planet for long—the average life span in America is rising, but still under eighty years—which frightens a hyperreal world. Death is a little too . . . real . . . a little too permanent. That's why the celebrity culture is so focused on youth. Botox. Antiaging clinics. Face creams.

Cosmetic surgery. Breast implants. Lip injections. Things that are all intended to trick the eye and keep us firmly planted in the world of hyperreality, a place, like Peter Pan's Neverland, where people never have to grow up.

But in hyperreality, people are disconnected not only from reality but also from each other. Individualism is king, and engaging in community at any deep level is increasingly uncommon. In fact, one of the perks of celebrity status is having the freedom to avoid the common people—or the freedom to avoid everyone. Money buys celebrities that privilege. No crowded Southwest flights for celebs, but rather, small, exclusive jets. No religions that involve dealing with people and working in soup kitchens, but, instead, personalized faiths that have more in common with getting a personal trainer than getting a personal calling.

The trouble with celebrity is that it pulls at something deep within us—and pulls us away from something deeper still.

- **Play DVD.**

- **Turn the page and follow along with the DVD.**

- **Discussion questions are at the end of the session.**

Week 2wo

The Trouble with Celebrity

Back to the Future

In Week One we explored how hyperreality is a juiced-up version of what life could be, sort of like a plastic Christmas tree. It looks like a real tree . . . until you get up close. But what does a real tree even look like? It's hard to even remember. In our culture, we're not encouraged to go off walking through the forest in search of the real thing, though. We're told that if we want to be happy, we need to move more fully into the hyperreal world and embrace its values. This leads to consumerism—the idea that happiness is found through the acquisition of things. And at its most insidious, consumerism sees the entire world as a commodity—including you: you're the product, and your body, the storefront.

Travel: Where the Grass Is Always Greener

When John Steinbeck wrote his travelogue, *Travels with Charley*, he remarked that almost everywhere he went, people were envious of his trip, because they, too, wanted to go somewhere—*anywhere*. People were restless. More than forty years after Steinbeck's famous road trip, people still want to go somewhere, except they're now acting on that restlessness. Today, travel is the new status symbol. At any given time, there are 250,000 Australians living in London, and 400,000 British living in Australia. If you want to make a good impression at a party, talk about the white-water

"The root of all evil is not money, it's boredom."

"People today hunger not for personal salvation . . . but for the feeling, the momentary illusion of personal well-being, health, and psychic security."

—Christopher Lasch

rafting trip you took in Zimbabwe or the camel ride you took in Jordan. In hyperreality, travel stories are a quick way to attain social status. Based on the way people react to travel, it would appear the grass is always greener on the other side. Going has become so popular that it's been suggested by some that *staying is the new going*. It's strange to think that something once as natural as *staying* is now considered to be countercultural.

Starbucks: "In the Business of Filling Souls"

Today, people collect experiences—a fact not lost on marketers and businesspeople. According to executives at Starbucks, the company is not just selling coffee; it's selling the Milanese coffee experience. And it's figured a way to package and sell that experience from Maine to Malaysia. In fact, CEO Howard Schultz has said that Starbucks is not just in the business of filling coffee cups but "in the business of filling souls." Think that's just marketing-speak? Not for Schultz. "No, I mean this is how we feel," Schultz told CBS's *60 Minutes* in 2006. "We're in the business of human connection and humanity, creating communities in a third place between home and work." In hyperreality, experience is the new gold standard, and businesses are rushing to provide just that.

Youth Is Everything

Youth culture changes faster than the weather. What's hot today will be cold tomorrow. Because teens have changing tastes and disposable income, marketers endlessly introduce new things for teens to buy. The music industry is perhaps the best example of this. Spend some time with the music charts from previous years, and you'll find names you haven't heard lately—or ever; artists who may be stocking grocery store shelves only a few years after their hit singles and Grammy nominations. That's not necessarily because they lacked talent—it's because they lacked the ability to reinvent themselves. Look at music artists with longevity, people such as Madonna. The Material Girl reinvented herself every year or two with different hairstyles, clothes, and musical styles, and as a result had a very long career and made big money. She knew how to feed the youth culture machine, instead of being chewed up by it.

There wasn't much of a youth culture prior to World War II, but today it can be broken down into three groups: teen, tween (middle school–aged kids), and pre-tween. And marketers are well aware of what buttons to push for each of these ages. *Seventeen* magazine, for example, is not aimed at girls who are seventeen—it's for tweens who want to be treated as teens. Meanwhile, teens barely old enough to drive are featured in music videos, dancing provocatively. This youth-focused marketing is so pervasive that it actually affects adults too.

"Forty is the new thirty."

—Courtney Cox

The Midlife Crisis . . . at Thirty

One of the hallmarks of hyperreality is that everything is accelerated. Little girls wear bikinis at age ten, boys plot sexual conquests at age twelve, and adults have midlife crises at age thirty. Yes, youth culture is affecting adults as well. Some examples of this new midlife crisis: the biggest consumers of video games are men in their thirties, the wardrobes of young mothers are indistinguishable from those of their daughters, and people are staying single longer—a sort of perpetual adolescence. Today, the slogan for adults is "You're only as old as you feel"—or as actress Courtney Cox says, "Forty is the new thirty."

Celebrity Culture

We're fascinated with celebrities—just glance at the magazines in the supermarket checkout aisle. There you'll learn how much so-and-so earns, who's sleeping with whom, and who looked best at the Golden Globe Awards. You'll also learn who looks good without their makeup and who needs more of it, which restaurant the A-listers are raving about, and where to buy a dress similar to the one Reese Witherspoon wore on the red carpet. What does this endless fascination with celebrity say about us?

"Given the advent of the Internet and reality television, a lot of kids think that fame is a realistic goal."

—Zena Burns

Whatever it says, our interest in celebrity culture cultivates this nagging feeling that our middle-class lives are somehow incomplete compared to those of the rich and famous—this in spite of the fact that much of the world lives on less than a few dollars a day. In fact, in the West, we are part of the richest and safest culture the world has ever known, but chatting with friends, you wouldn't think so (even though many of us possess the latest gadgets, rent or buy in fashionable areas, regularly travel overseas, and wear current fashions). But we don't compare ourselves with the vast majority of the world—those in need of clean water and basic medical care. We compare ourselves with the exceedingly wealthy. And with that as our measuring stick, we usually come up feeling inadequate and discontented.

Me, Myself, and I

Hyperreality has its foundations in Western enlightenment thinking—a worldview in which the individual reigns supreme. The West has always put an emphasis on personal autonomy. America personifies this sort of thinking. Just watch any old Western movie and you'll see a one-on-one gun battle between the solitary hero and the solitary villain. Or look at the "American road trip"—the idea that anyone can get on the open road and just go. Unlike other cultures, which stress mass transportation, America prizes individual transportation. Today, our culture's idea of individualism is so extreme that former president John F. Kennedy's "ask not what your country can do for you, but what you can do for your country" speech hardly resonates with most people. In the West, governments have become servants of the people. The idea of sacrificing yourself for the greater good is almost entirely foreign to the Western person—something that has affected our view of commitment. In hyperreality, it could be said that the only important commitment is the one you have to your own happiness.

Strangers in a Strange Land

By the rivers of Babylon we sat and wept
    when we remembered Zion, *our home, so far away.*
On the branches of the willow trees we hung our harps
    and hid our hearts from the enemy.
And the men that surrounded us made demands
    that we clap our hands and sing—
    songs of joy from days gone by,
    songs from home.
Such cruel men taunted us—
    haunted our memories.
How could we sing a song about the Eternal One in a land so foreign,
    while still tormented, brokenhearted, homesick?
    Please don't make us sing this song.
O Jerusalem, even still,
    please don't escape my memory.
    I treasure you and your songs,
    even as I hide my harp from the enemy.
And if I can't remember, may I never sing a song again;
    may I never play well again,
    for what use would it be
If I don't remember home
    as my source of joy.

—Psalm 137:1–6 (Voice)

This scripture recounts a time when the Jews were taken from their homeland and placed in Babylonian captivity—the modern-day equivalent of being kidnapped from Mongolia and dumped in the middle of New York City. Talk about culture shock. How do you preserve your heritage, your faith, in the middle of the most powerful place on earth? How do you worship the *unseen* amid the *seen*? How do you preserve family traditions in a place more capable of changing you than you changing it? Certainly the Jews must have asked themselves these questions. But we must ask the same questions today. Though we're not technically enslaved—we're the freest people to ever walk the face of the earth—our thoughts are less under our control than we might imagine. That is, until we begin to knock down the walls of hyperreality and change how we think about the world. And we must. We can't live in hyperreality. It's not real.

Discussion Questions

1 What stood out to you in this session? Go around the group and share.

2 What personal questions did this session raise for you?

3 What experiences carry the highest status among you or your friends?

4 When have you found yourself telling stories of your possessions or experiences in order to elicit positive reactions from others?

Discussion

5 How do you see the people around you using experience to create meaning? When have you done this yourself?

6 How do you feel about getting old? Are you afraid of it? Why? If so, how do you see this fear manifesting itself in how you live your life?

7 How much discontentment could be attributed to comparing yourself to others?

8 To whom do you compare yourself? Are these people in any way worse off than you?

Discussion

9 Do you live with the constant feeling that your life is boring? If so, why?

10 In what ways have you seen individualism affecting our culture?

11 How does "self" rule in your life?

12 When do you feel lonely?

The Trouble with Entertainment

An Introduction to Week Three

There are a lot of things in life that aren't all that entertaining. Mowing the lawn. Doing the laundry. Mopping the floor. Paying bills. Putting the groceries away. These are part of the real world, yet hyperreality would have you believe that doing your own everyday chores is an indication that your life is headed in the wrong direction. But that just isn't real life. Only the obscenely rich can have someone else handle all of life's mundane details. Toil is a fact of life.

However, in hyperreality, if you're not being entertained—if you're not experiencing euphoria throughout the day—you're somehow missing the boat. Of course, this is a lie. Even for the rich and famous, the overseas trip must come to an end—and even if the trip could last forever, that sexy, overseas locale would eventually become plain and boring, prompting another search for stimulation. As the saying goes, "Wherever you go, there you are"; or in other words, if you feel empty now, the new city you're moving to or the vacation destination you're aiming for won't improve things for long.

Stimulation is synonymous with hyperreality. You can watch television on your cell phone, view movies on your computer, and play video games on just about any electronic device. In hyperreality, the TV is always on, the phone is always ringing, and there are always text messages to respond to. The hope is that this busyness will keep you from any connection to reality, because, in the words of that early '90s movie, "reality bites." And it's true: reality is not always fun—but that's how life is sometimes. Real peace can only be achieved when one can learn to face reality, rather than trying to sidestep it, escape it, or transcend it. Facing the hard times, while it may not initially sound appealing, can be more deeply rewarding than living what we might call the "good life"; that is, hyperreality.

The problem is, we can and do experience our moments of hyperreality—those times when we get backstage passes to the big concert, stand in Times Square on New Year's Eve, or ride in a limo to some trendy nightclub. But the illusion of hyperreality can't sustain itself—the feeling never lasts. Yet instead of accepting this fact, some people try to create as many hyperreal moments as possible. These are the folks you'll find at a concert, a club, a birthday party, a bar, or some other exciting event—*every night*. It's an understandable way to live because, again, at first glance reality just doesn't measure up to hyperreality.

Reality means listening to long-winded speeches to determine who to vote for in an election, reading an entire book in order to do well on a college exam, or chopping vegetables for a salad. It means going to bed early because you feel a cold coming on. But what does hyperreality offer? Seven-second sound bites of the political speech on CNN, *Cliff's Notes* for that hard-to-read novel, and precut vegetables in the supermarket veggie aisle. It's just like reality, only better. Yet taking these shortcuts leaves us worse off than if we had accepted that work is a necessary part of life.

We've come to believe that life should be like a television show with a breezy beginning, middle, and end. But real life doesn't come in prepackaged, easy-to-digest, twenty-two-minute bits. It's messy, tedious, and usually painful. And despite hyperreality's never-ending claims of perpetual youth and vitality, we all eventually die. In light of death, how much of what hyperreality tries to offer is really all that important?

The fact is we just can't be entertained our entire lives. And even if we could, we'd miss out on so much: the satisfaction that comes from tough, manual labor; the feeling of achievement we get from writing a well-researched term paper; the enlargement of our souls after a day of reflective silence; and most important, the wholeness that comes from living not in hyperreality but in God's reality—a place where everything is kept in context, everything in its proper place.

Author Richard Rohr wrote, "I suspect we are actually stunted and paralyzed by having too many options. We are no longer the developed world; we are the overdeveloped world." And that just might be another definition of hyperreal: overdeveloped. In hyperreality, we are overstimulated, overdeveloped, oversaturated, and overwhelmed.

- **Play DVD.**

- **Turn the page and follow along with the DVD.**

- **Discussion questions are at the end of the session.**

The Trouble with Entertainment

Pulling Weeds and Taking out the Trash

For the last two sessions, we've looked at how hyperreality shapes our view of the world. We broke it apart and looked at some of its traits and how those traits impact our lives. There were some problems, though, and it forced us to ask just how well hyperreality is able to provide happy, fulfilling lives. Not very, it seems. Not only does it take more and more stimulation to keep us engaged and intrigued, but we also seem less and less fulfilled the more we chase after hyperreal experiences. Another problem with hyperreality is that we don't live there; we live here, in reality, the real world—pulling weeds, taking out the trash, picking the kids up from school, and cleaning the kitchen. But then we go to the grocery store, hear that pop music playing, see the fluorescent lights

shining, and look at the glossy gossip magazines—while standing behind a mother and her screaming baby at the checkout. And we think, again, for the millionth time, that if we could just get that product or improve our sex lives or find cool friends or buy that luxury car or go on vacation, we could escape this boring, average world.

I guess, deep down, we all wish our lives could be as glamorous as the people we see in the magazines. But they can't. See, the problem with hyperreality is that it tricks us. We see the girl in the magazine as having it all—she's beautiful, interesting, wealthy, famous, desirable—when in reality she is just a girl, deeply troubled, imprisoned by fame, and as discontented and disillusioned as you feel while looking at the gorgeous photo of her basking in the flash of the paparazzi's cameras and wearing "perfect" clothes.

Hyperreality offers us the honeymoon period of a relationship and says your whole life can and should be like this—but it can't. Honeymoons always end. New cars get old. Favorite songs fade to the back of our iTunes playlists. New sweaters get tattered and end up in attics.

"When we have no project to finish, no friend to visit, no book to read, no television to watch . . . and when we are left all alone by ourselves, we are brought so close to the revelation of our basic human aloneness and so afraid of experiencing an all-pervasive sense of loneliness that we will do anything to get busy again and continue the game which makes us believe that everything is fine after all."

—Henry Nouwen

We Have to Go Home

Our culture is telling us we have to move all of our lives into hyperreality, and yet here we are, realizing we can't do that, because we live in the world of reality. The tricky part is that occasionally there are moments when reality and hyperreality intersect. But these moments don't last. We always have to return to reality. Take, for example, a night of drinking in a club. There's a moment during the evening when everything is great—attractive people everywhere, lights flashing, muscles relaxing, confidence soaring. This is hyperreality. But then there's the next morning: head pounding, conscience reprimanding, and sunlight stinging our tired eyes. We're back in reality. People can spend their entire lives trying to prolong hyperreality, but they—and we—have to come back to the real world. The club always closes. The lights always stop flashing. We always have to go home.

> "To increase their capacity for consumption, consumers must never be allowed to rest. They need to be kept forever awake and on the alert, constantly exposed to new temptations and so remain . . . in a state of perpetual suspicion and steady disaffection."
>
> —Zygmunt Bauman

Be Dissatisfied—or Else

One of the things hyperreality teaches is that if we don't live superstar lives, we have no life at all. In fact, our whole economy is based on this dissatisfaction. Can you imagine if everyone was content with what they owned? The global economy would grind to a halt. So it's really in the best interest of brands and marketers to foster a sense of dissatisfaction within us. It's so critical that consumers keep consuming that there's even something called "planned obsolesce" in which manufacturers actually make products in such a way that they will break down after a certain period of time. So even if you're satisfied with what you have, you will still need to buy a new one soon. This happens with all sorts of electronic and mechanical products, from computers to automobiles. Car manufacturers actually have the ability to produce vehicles that will drive for 500,000 miles or more, but instead, they manufacture automobiles to break down long before that. In hyperreality, you must keep buying.

We live in an "I will be happy when . . ." culture. So no matter how affluent or comfortable our lives are, we will always be looking over our shoulders. This is an addictive, downward spiral. Hyperreality doesn't allow us to ever be satisfied, and without satisfaction, we will never experience contentment or true meaning.

Shouldn't Life Always Be Fun?

In Thornton Wilder's Pulitzer Prize–winning play, *Our Town*, the main character, Emily, dies but is given the chance to go back and relive a day from her childhood. The advice Emily receives is to relive an ordinary day—the idea being that real life is lived in the mundane, not in those hyperreal moments that are the exceptions, not the norm. Initially overjoyed at having a chance to live again, Emily soon becomes despondent at how much people take for granted. "Doesn't anyone ever realize life while they live it? Every, every minute?" Emily asks, to which the narrator responds, "No. Saints and poets, maybe; they do some." Wilder's point was that every moment—especially those normal, everyday ones—is infused with wonder and meaning. This is the antithesis of hyperreality.

Like the characters in *Our Town*, we, too, fail to see how important everyday moments in life are. We fail to hear one another, to look each other in the eye, to take joy in the simple things. Most of us have grown up exposed to millions of ads and thousands of videos, with their quick cuts. We live in a world where mobile phones act as iPods, iPods as televisions, televisions as computers, and computers as *everything*. All of this sends the message that we should be entertained all the time. We've actually developed the notion that we have the *right* to be entertained. But large parts of life—significant parts—are not entertaining. Life is washing the dishes, resting, even cleaning the toilet.

I Hate My Job

People in television shows often have jobs that are glamorous and exciting. They're always wearing the best clothes, having lunch at the perfect restaurants, staying in expensive hotels, drinking things we can't pronounce, and being continually rewarded for their labors with lots of money and acclaim. They get to travel the world, become best friends with their colleagues, and have a fun time while doing it all. In fact, unless you're watching *The Office*, you don't see people photocopying for hours, or just sitting at their desks and shuffling papers. That's too mundane, too *unsatisfying*.

In survey after survey, today's young adults say they are dissatisfied with their jobs, but what are they really expecting their jobs to do for them? Too many, it seems, are looking for work to fulfill all of their needs—emotional, financial, and spiritual. But most people—ourselves included—will never achieve all of this through work. More often than not, our jobs won't be exciting or wonderful—they will just help us pay the bills. Hyperreality makes that look like a bad thing, but work is sometimes simply that: work.

"When asked to identify themselves today, people commonly refer to their career, job title, employer, or educational achievements. This response illustrates how the culture of modernity roots a person's identity in one's achievements and place in the social order, especially the economic social order. What identifies people is their function—what they do rather than their character or personal qualities."

—Craig Van Gelder

(Hyper) Reality Check

After high school, I spent some time in Los Angeles. I lived in a low-income area populated by mostly Cambodian people, a place fraught with violence. People would go to sleep to the sound of gunshots and wake up to a decaying urban scene of drugs and poverty. It was one of the worst areas I'd ever seen. But when one Cambodian family invited me to their cramped apartment for dinner, I asked them what it was like to live in such a place—a place where people bought crack in the alleys. The father replied that he was incredibly grateful to God to live in the United States when his relatives in Cambodia struggle so much. I couldn't believe what I was hearing: my version of hell was their heaven. I had become so used to the comfortable lifestyle of the West that I didn't realize people in other parts of the world lived in such poverty.

Much of the world lives in conditions we would call hellish. While the September 11 attacks killed nearly 3,000 people, experts believe that nearly 30,000 children die *every day* from preventable conditions. In fact, according to the World Bank, in 2001, about 1.1 billion humans lived off of less than $1 (U.S.) per day. Preventable and treatable diseases, such as AIDS, malaria, and tuberculosis kill thousands of Africans daily. All over the world people are suffering and dying from poor sanitation, disease, war, forced prostitution, and slavery—yet many young adults feel that they are not doing so well because they can't regularly travel or buy the most up-to-date electronic gadgets. You can spend all day wishing you had the lifestyle of Brad Pitt or Paris Hilton—but if you live in the West, you've won the cosmic lottery compared to the rest of the world.

Rich and Depressed

Antidepressants are now the most prescribed drugs in the U.S., and according to one expert, 25 percent of American adults will have a "major depressive episode" at some point in life. However, Americans aren't alone. China has made major gains in affluence over the past decade, yet experts say that along with a rise in personal income has been an increase in suicide rates. In fact, suicide is now the single biggest killer of young adults in urban China. How do we explain the huge prevalence of depression in countries with so much wealth? We can only conclude

"It is the most basic human loneliness that threatens us and is so hard to face. Too often we will do everything possible to avoid the confrontation with the experience of being alone, and sometimes we are able to create the most ingenious devices to prevent ourselves from being reminded of this condition."

—Henri Nouwen

that consumerism's promise that we can buy our way to happiness is not working. It would appear that frenzied activity and wealth do not buy peace of mind.

A Pain-Free Existence?

We have been shaped so much by television. For many of us, television has been our teacher, comforter, and constant companion through life. We may not remember much about third grade, but we can recall all sorts of details about the cartoons and TV shows we used to watch.

Television isn't a bad thing, but it often paints an inaccurate picture of how life works. Often, a TV show is based on a character that is suddenly faced with a crisis or problem. But by the end of the thirty-minute episode, the crisis has been resolved. Real life isn't like that. We rarely see a show whose main character has been sexually abused and then has to live with that forever—never able to form lasting relationships as a result. In fact, we rarely see pain of any type portrayed as a part of everyday life.

But it is.

Insignificance, Aging, and Death

Hyperreality tells us that by making the right consumer choices, becoming popular, looking beautiful, and creating an exciting portfolio of experiences, we can attain significance. We're told that youth is everything, and aging, something to fear. But let's be honest: we can't fight time. Everyone who came before us—no matter how beautiful, how robust, how fit, how energetic, how many vitamins they took—has died, and we will too. Our bodies are aging and breaking down. We are getting older. Even those of us who eat well, work out, use skin creams, get eight hours of sleep, and drink lots of water are aging. We will one day pass away, only to be remembered by a few friends and family. Of all the lies hyperreality tells, perhaps the biggest is that we're invincible. But we're not. Death will come—sooner or later. And how we face death is very important. To run from it is to become enslaved by it. If we're going to be free, we need to realize that we're not on this planet for long.

Read Ecclesiastes 5.

The verses you've just read are from the book of Ecclesiastes—a strange book that woefully tells us that life is short, pleasure is fleeting, and death is inevitable. But Ecclesiastes also hints at another reality: God's reality. If we're going to understand life, we have to understand the three spheres of *hyperreality*, *reality*, and *God's reality*. And Ecclesiastes—which not coincidentally was written by one of the wealthiest men of the ancient world, a man who had everything he could ever want—comes to the conclusion that if we are to live lives of meaning, we have to trust God and bring our lives into *his* reality, where everything is as it should be.

Discussion

Discussion Questions

1. What stood out to you in this session? Go around the group and share.

2 What would you like to change about yourself?

3 How has advertising affected the things you would like to change about yourself?

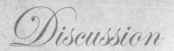
Discussion

4 What is your "I will be happy when . . ." scenario?

5 How happy are you with your career situation at the moment? What do you think most people want from a career? How realistic do you think this is?

6 How well have you begun to plan for the shortness of life?

7 How prepared do you feel to deal with the large portions of personal pain that life brings?

Discussion

8 How have your education and Western worldview equipped you (or not equipped you) to deal with the reality of pain in your life?

9 When you are at home, with no distractions and nothing to do, how do you feel?

10 To what extent do you feel the need to be constantly entertained? Why?

The Promise of God's Reality

An Introduction to Week Four

These days, the term "God's reality" may sound like more of an oxymoron than anything else. Popular books on atheism portray those who believe in God as, at best, weak-minded and, at worst, dangerous people who use faith to justify the worst of atrocities. God is seen as anything but real, while the negative actions of his followers, all too real.

Add to this the notion of hyperreality, which says we attain happiness by having the right connections, looks, possessions, careers, and experiences. It's as if God has been forced out of the building, and who has time to go looking for him? After all, there's a movie to watch, a plane to catch, or an e-mail to type. We have things to do.

For many of us, it's just as the Samuel Beckett play *Waiting for Godot* suggests: even if we were looking for God (or in Beckett's play, waiting for Godot), he never shows up, because God's not real—he's just another story to help us sleep at night. If this is true, we must seize the day and cram in all the pleasure we can, for as Alain de Botton wrote, "When a belief in the next world is interpreted as a childish and scientifically impossible opiate, the pressure to succeed and fulfill oneself will inevitably be inflamed by the awareness that there is only a single and frighteningly brief opportunity to do so."

Yet, what if there is another reality? What if God isn't some fairy-tale deity, but actually the essence of reality—a perfect being with a plan for all of life? What if he really lives and functions in a world where everything belongs, and in its proper context too? Maybe there is an alternative to hyperreality, one that embraces not only life but the bad parts of life that hyperreality tries to avoid.

And maybe there is a heaven—not one filled with boring church music and fluffy clouds, but one that's exciting and available to us here and now—as well as later. Let's set aside our past experiences with religion and look at the Bible with fresh eyes, beginning with the Old Testament—or what Bono appropriately calls "an action movie" filled with "blood, car chases, evacuations, a lot of special effects"—and ending with the New Testament, a story of redemption, prophetic fulfillment, and heaven on earth.

In walking through the biblical story, we'll explore the overarching narrative of creation, from the garden of Eden to God's decision to choose a people of his own; his people's rebellion (a regular event) to God's forgiveness (a regular event); and God's plan to make all things new, and how exactly he will accomplish that. And in looking at this narrative, we'll see if we can experience true meaning by asking ourselves if the Bible's claims are true—if, when we enter into God's reality, it truly is like seeing everything for the first time. We'll ask ourselves if real meaning is found, not by going after hyperreality, but by aligning our reality with God's.

- Play DVD.
- Turn the page and follow along with the DVD.
- Discussion questions are at the end of the session.

The Promise of God's Reality

God's Future

In our last session, we looked at how our culture encourages us to run away from some of the key issues of life—things such as death, injustice, suffering, and pain. By chasing after hyperreality we miss so much of life, and we insulate ourselves from anything unpleasant. We also looked at how the Bible hints at another reality, something called *God's reality*. But before we investigate what that is, we need to address the fact that when most of us think of God's reality, we think of heaven—and when we think of heaven, we think of the word *boring*. And indeed, virtually every movie reinforces the afterlife as mind-numbingly

repetitive, like strumming the same tune on a harp again and again, or making a never-ending list of synonyms for the word *happy*. But just how biblical is our view of God's future for us? And how scriptural is our view of God's reality—heaven?

"When a belief in the next world is interpreted as a childish and scientifically impossible opiate, the pressure to succeed and fulfill oneself will inevitably be inflamed by the awareness that there is only a single and frighteningly brief opportunity to do so. Earthly achievement can no longer be seen as an overture to what one may realize in another world, they are the sum total of all one will ever be."

—Alain de Botton

More than a Church Service

It's not hard to see why most people don't like the idea of heaven—after all, what images come to mind when you think of eternity with God? Clouds? Angels? A never-ending church service, where you sing hymns billions of times in a row? The idea of delaying gratification for some kind of heavenly reward is laughable to a hyperreal world, and even more so with cliché images such as these. Surely God must have a more robust plan for our future than the heavenly scenarios most of us have grown up believing.

To get an accurate view of heaven, we need to look at the Bible, an anthology written over thousands of years by dozens of authors, but a book that maintains a coherent thread throughout: God's dream for the world. As followers of Jesus, we need to place ourselves within that story in order to better understand it, as well as to understand how starkly God's reality differs from hyperreality.

Things Are Good, Until . . .

God created the world as a place of goodness, not only for humanity but also for all of creation. In Genesis we learn that God placed Adam and Eve in a garden and provided everything they needed. They didn't even have to kill animals for food—they ate plants.

Better still, Adam and Eve walked with God himself in the cool of the evening; God was in communion with his people, and they were in communion with him and with each other. There was harmony.

And then something happened.

In the center of the garden were two trees, one of which was known as the Tree of Knowledge of Good and Evil. It was from that tree that Adam and Eve were told not to eat—and, of course, the tree from which they ultimately ate. This helps us understand why the world is not as it should be—a reference point for understanding why there is pain, war, suffering, and conflict. We are no longer in communion with nature, each other, or God.

Adam and Eve may have been the first humans to disobey God, but they were not the last. Adam and Eve's children were born into the fallen world, and their children had children, and their children had more children, and so on. Before long, the world was populated with corrupt and violent people, and God grieved when he saw the wickedness of mankind. He saw no option left but to wipe the earth clean of all creatures and start new. So God sent a great flood that destroyed all men and animals, saving only Noah—a righteous and blameless man—and his family, and two of every animal, in order to repopulate the earth after the flood.

Despite the world's disobedience, God was not finished with it. He waited until just the right time, and he did something extraordinary: he called a nomadic couple named Abraham and Sarah—neither powerful nor extraordinary—to birth a nation. And though they had been unable to have children for decades, God promised Abraham and Sarah that he would make them parents of the nation Israel—even though they were ninety and one hundred years old! Their task: to live as God's people among other nations, and to lead them to understand God's plan for the world.

Oppression and Salvation

God's promise came true: Abraham and Sarah gave birth to a great nation. But being nomadic and surrounded by more powerful nations, God's people were eventually enslaved by the Egyptian empire, forced to become workhorses for the Egyptians.

But in due time, God sent a messenger, a man named Moses, to challenge the might of Egypt and lead his people out of slavery and into a land he would give them—a place known as the promised land.

Moses was an unlikely candidate for this important job: not only was he shy, but he was also a poor speaker. Yet with God behind him, Moses ultimately confronted the world's most powerful leader and won his people's freedom. A few plagues sent by God didn't exactly hurt either. Blood, lice, flies . . . you know the story. It was a long road trip for the Israelites, though—forty years, to be exact, through the desert—and all the while, they were constantly asking, "Are we there yet? Are we there yet? Are we there yet?" They were so impatient. And worse, they were rebellious and easily corrupted, time and again. God had ordered them to destroy the inhabitants of the land they were to possess. Instead, they merged with them, giving in to their culture and actually worshiping their idols instead of God.

God still didn't give up on them: he provided them with both a system of laws—the Ten Commandments—and a system of worship, designed to fashion them into a holy people, set apart from other nations.

But the Israelites were incredibly human, very much like us, and they consistently resisted God's dreams and ignored his commands to look after the poor, the foreigners, and the refugees. And even though God had told them that *he* was their king, eventually they asked for—and got—another king, so they could be "like everyone else." Soon, they were virtually indistinguishable from the nations around them.

It appeared that God's dreams were in ruins, and that his people, though no longer slaves in Egypt, were still slaves—to their own passions and desires. So God sent prophets, who implored the people to turn their hearts back to him and away from power, oppression, greed, and idolatry. The prophets—Amos, Hosea, and Isaiah, among others—warned the people that if they stayed on their current path, they would reap negative consequences—that whole "you reap what you sow" thing. And sure enough, the Israelites were again overrun by a more powerful nation.

Slaves Again

Eventually, another foreign power, the Babylonians, invaded Israel and enslaved its leading citizens. The temple in Jerusalem, built by King Solomon as the place to worship God, was destroyed, and God's people were sent into not only geographical exile but spiritual exile as well. The prophet Ezekiel recorded the pain of being overrun, describing it as God's glory leaving (Ezekiel 8). It was a dark period in Israel's history. And years later, even when the Jews were finally allowed to return to their homeland, more powerful neighbors repeatedly invaded them. They were the world's whipping boy. To make matters worse, the temple was still in ruins, as was the spiritual condition of the Israelites. It seemed as though Israel couldn't get a break, and its people certainly didn't do themselves any favors either.

Looking for a Savior

During this spiritual exile, the prophets continued to demand that the Jews return to their first love: God. Mixed in with these prophetic warnings was a deep desire for the emergence of a Messiah, who, according to Jewish theology, would defeat their oppressors and establish Israel as a kingdom of righteousness—a kingdom that would lead the world in an age of absolute peace and prosperity and would even see God return to his temple. And after hundreds of years of silence from God, this "dream king" *did* emerge—in a way no one ever imagined.

God in a Barn

The Messiah arrived in the strangest of ways—as a baby, surrounded by filth and animals in the small town of Bethlehem. Jesus was born to a virgin mother and a carpenter father, and people whispered about him early in life—especially when he went to Jerusalem as a boy and lectured in the temple. There, the rabbis were amazed by his insight and learning. But things got quiet again, and we read no more about him until he was thirty, when he began his public ministry.

For the next three years, Jesus walked among people, healing them, teaching in public, traveling from town to town. He hung out with regular people, including a group of fishermen who became his followers. His actions pointed people toward the heart of God instead of simply being part of the religious establishment, Jesus was an agent of change, reaching out to the marginalized and calling the religious leaders to account for their hypocrisy, hard-heartedness, and self-righteousness.

Jesus didn't bring about the peace and prosperity that people imagined he would; he *was* that peace and prosperity—and still folks were disappointed in him. What's more, Jesus acknowledged that he and God were one and the same, and this upset more than a few people. He was ultimately killed by the powers-that-be—not only the religious establishment but also the Roman authorities, who feared a revolt. His execution by crucifixion was the most heinous crime ever perpetrated against a human being—especially since this human was God in the flesh. Jesus Christ died a criminal's death and was placed in a borrowed tomb—becoming the once-for-all sacrifice that would pay for the sins of all humanity.

But death couldn't keep him down. On the third day, Jesus rose to defeat death and evil and confirm his extraordinary claim to be God in human form. He was seen—alive—by Mary, a woman out of whom he had cast demons. He was seen by two of his followers. And finally, he was seen by the Eleven, those faithful disciples who had not betrayed him. His resurrection could not be refuted.

Jesus had spent three years making God's wishes known to his disciples. But now, once more, he commissioned them to go out into the world and proclaim the good news—God's reality—to everyone. Then, before their very eyes, Jesus of Nazareth was caught up into heaven.

Born of a virgin. Crucified. Raised from the dead. And ascended. God had intervened in our world, marrying his reality with ours—forever.

Understanding God's Reality— and Dream

If we really want to understand God's reality, we need to understand Jesus. Jesus came not just to die for us but also to redeem the whole world. It's as if everything had been put in its wrong spot—milk in the cupboards, socks in the sink, shoes on the couch—and Jesus came and set everything in its proper place. But more than that, Jesus came to give us life—and life "more abundantly" (John 10:10 KJV). And it was clearly a life that people knew little about—a life that still confounds the world today.

Just look at the way Jesus loved and served others. He treated everyone equally, whether they were poor or rich, weak or strong, young or old. How Jesus lived his life became the blueprint for how we are to live out God's idea for the future. He has a dream for this world, and our deepest desires and needs are met through that dream—if we choose to live in his reality. The good news is God doesn't expect us to move our lives into his reality through our own human effort; he meets us along the way.

One day, Scripture tells us, Jesus will return, just as he came, and the whole world will be enveloped by God's reality. Justice will flow like a river, and peace will reign supreme. All terrorism, war, hatred, and poverty will end. In fact, Isaiah 2:4 says the weapons of the world will be smashed into plows to produce food. Amazing! All pain and suffering will cease. Death will no longer have a hold on creation, and humans will relate to one another—finally—through unconditional love. In fact, everything that humanity has ever yearned for will come true.

God's Future: Our Present

The revolutionary thing about God's future is that it reaches out and grabs us in the present. It's not some kind of tantalizing reward that's always going to be just ahead of us—it's a moving stream that meets us where we are and once we get in, it pulls us along, changing the way we act and think.

When Jesus began his public ministry, he proclaimed the year of the Lord's favor. On one level, he was talking about himself—he was living proof of God's favor upon humanity—but on another level, he was saying that there were parts of heaven, of God's reality, available for us to touch right now, at this very moment. We catch glimpses of it when we have a delicious meal, see a great film, talk with a friend, or enjoy nature. And that's just the present. What about the future?

God's future is not fully revealed to us—only partly so—but as we seek to bring his reality to planet earth, it's as if we put on a pair of divine glasses. And what happens? We see everything differently—we see as he sees. And when we see through God's eyes, we begin to embrace his reality and live it out. How? By helping the refugee, explaining God's plan to those who haven't heard, feeding the poor, visiting the prisoner, and loving our enemies. As our actions bring change to our world, we get a glimpse of God's reality for the future. And it is when we begin to live in this kind of reality—not hyperreality—that we discover peace. All the bad things don't disappear, but our lives become enveloped with a very different way of viewing the world.

Happiness and Meaning

Ah . . . a life of happiness and meaning. That's what we all want, isn't it? Yet burying the tough things in life and embracing instead the hyperreal dream of perpetual youth, wealth, beauty, status, and tantalizing experiences won't get us there. True happiness and meaning can only be obtained and *re*tained one way: by embracing God and making him the center of our world. God *is* the meaning. He is where we will find meaning. Then, and only then, we begin to see what true living is.

Discussion

Week 4our

Discussion Questions

1 How do you imagine heaven? Is your view of heaven based on Scripture, or is it shaped more by Hollywood's "harps and clouds" version of the afterlife? Why do you feel this way?

2 How does the sweeping story of the Bible change how you think of heaven / God's reality? How do Jesus' life and actions point us to what heaven / God's reality will be like?

3 Compare and contrast God's reality with hyperreality. How are they different?

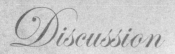

Discussion

4 Did the forbidden fruit in the garden of Eden represent the same false promise that hyperreality represents for us today? Why or why not?

5 Does God's reality make sense to you? Does it help you understand life better than hyperreality does? Why or why not?

6 What do the conditions in which Jesus was born—essentially, a dirty stable—say about God's reality?

7 How do you experience heaven in the here and now in your daily life? What things could you be doing to bring heaven on earth to those around you?

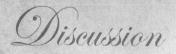

Discussion

8 How can God's future be available both now and later?

9 Give examples from your life of times when you have gone after hyperreality. Then give examples of the times you have embraced God's reality. How do the experiences differ? Did living in God's reality produce peace?

QUOTED RESOURCES

Assayas, Michka, *Bono*. New York: Riverhead Trade, 2006. U2. "Even Better than the Real Thing," *Achtung Baby* [album]. Island, 1991.

Bauman, Zygmunt. *Globalization: The Human Consequences*. New York: Columbia University Press, 1998.

Burns, Zena. As quoted in the *New York Times* (NYTimes.com), "MTV's 'Super Sweet 16' Gives a Sour Pleasure." Article by Lola Ogunnaike, April 26, 2006, http://www.nytimes.com/2006/04/26/arts/television/26swee.html.

Center for Action and Contemplation. *Richard Rohr's Daily Reflection for Wednesday, October 24, 2007*. http://cacradicalgrace.org.

de Botton, Alain. *Status Anxiety*. London: Penguin, 2004.

Featherstone, Mike. *Consumer Culture and Postmodernism*. London: Sage, 1991.

Hilton, Paris and Merle Ginsberg. *Your Heiress Diary: Confess It All to Me*. Milsons Point, Australia: Random House, 2005.

Kumar, Krishan. As quoted in *The New Fontana Dictionary of Modern Thought*, eds. Alan Bullock & Stephen Trombley. London: HarperCollins, 1999.

Lasch, Christopher. *The Culture of Narcissism: American Life in an Age of Diminishing Expectations*. New York: Warner Books, 1979.

Nouwen, Henri. *Reaching Out: The Three Movements of the Spiritual Life*. New York: Image Books, 1975.

Schultz, Howard. As quoted in *Howard Schultz: The Star of Starbucks*. Article by Tom Anderson, April 23, 2006, http://www.cbsnews.com/stories/2006/04/21/60minutes/main1532246.shtml.

Storkey, Alan. As quoted in *Christ and Consumerism: A Critical Analysis of the Spirit of the Age*, eds. C. Bartholomew and T. Moritz. Carlisle: Paternoster, 2000.

U2. "Even Better than the Real Thing," *Achtung Baby* [album]. Island, 1991.

Van Gelder, Craig. As quoted in *Missional Church: A Vision for the Sending of the Church in North America*, ed. Darrell L. Guder. Grand Rapids: Eerdmans, 1998.

Learn more about following Jesus in a World of Plastic Promises

In *The Trouble With Paris DVD Study*, pastor Mark Sayers showed us how the lifestyles of most young actually work *against* a life of meaning and happiness to sabotage their faith. Now you can dig deeper into these issues. In *The Trouble With Paris* book, Sayers expands upon the themes of the DVD study and shows how a fresh understanding of God's intention for our world is the true path to happiness, fulfillment, and meaning.

$14.99
ISBN 9780849919992

Published by
THOMAS NELSON™
Since 1798
www.thomasnelson.com

Notes

Notes